The story of
the two brothers

Story by Penny Frank

Illustrated by John Haysom

The Bible tells us how God sent his Son Jesus to show us what God is like and how we can belong to God's kingdom.

This is a story Jesus told to show that God is always ready to forgive people who are sorry for disobeying him.

You can find this story in your own Bible, in Luke's Gospel, chapter 15.

Copyright © 1987 Lion Publishing

Published by
Lion Publishing plc
Sandy Lane West, Oxford, England
ISBN 0 85648 765 1
ISBN 0 7459 1785 2 (paperback)
Lion Publishing Corporation
1705 Hubbard Avenue, Batavia, Illinois 60510, USA
ISBN 0 85648 765 1
Albatross Books Pty Ltd
PO Box 320, Sutherland, NSW 2232, Australia
ISBN 0 86760 550 2
ISBN 0 7324 0105 4 (paperback)

First edition 1987, reprinted 1987, 1988 , 1990
Paperback edition 1989

British Library Cataloguing in Publication Data

Frank, Penny
    The story of the two brothers. – (The
    Lion Story Bible; 40)
    1. Jesus Christ – Teachings – Juvenile
    literature 2. Bible stories, English –
    N.T. Gospels
    I. Title II. Haysom, John
    232.9'54 BS2416
    ISBN 0-85648-765-1
    ISBN 0-7459-1785-2 (paperback)

Printed in Yugoslavia

Library of Congress Cataloging in Publication Data

Frank, Penny.
    The story of the two brothers.
    (The Lion Story Bible; 40)
    1. Prodigal son (Parable) – Juvenile
    literature. 2. Bible stories, English –
    N.T. Luke. [1. Prodigal son (Parable)
    2. Parables. 3. Bible stories – N.T.]
    I. Haysom, John, ill. II. Title.
    III. Series: Frank, Penny. Lion Story
    Bible; 40.
    BT378.P8F69 1987 226'.409505
    86-4701
    ISBN 0-85648-765-1
    ISBN 0-7459-1785-2 (paperback)

The teachers of God's Law did not like the kind of people Jesus mixed with.

'He goes out of his way to welcome the worst people you could think of,' they grumbled one day.

So Jesus told them this story.

There was once a farmer who was very rich. He had two sons who worked hard for him on his farm.

The sons knew that when their father died the farm would be shared between them. They did not want their father to die, but they were looking forward to being rich.

The younger son said to his father, 'Why can't I have my share now. It's silly to have to wait for you to die before I can be rich.'

The father loved them both very much and he wanted them to be happy. So he shared out his farm between them.

Instead of working hard, the younger son looked at his part of the farm and said, 'What's the use of all these fields and barns? If I sell them, I'll have money to spend.'

So the younger son sold his part of the farm and set off to seek his fortune.

The elder son stayed at home and worked hard on his farm with his father.

The younger son went away to a big city. He had never been anywhere like that before.

There was so much food and wine.

There were comfortable inns and lots of expensive clothes to buy.

When the young men in the city saw how much money the younger son had, they were very happy to be his friends. They all enjoyed spending the money.

One morning, the younger son woke up. After he had dressed and had his breakfast he began to plan the day. Everything he planned to do would cost some money, so he looked in his money-bag.

It was empty!

The younger son told his friends, 'We have spent all my money. What shall I do now?'

The friends just laughed and went off together. He never saw them again.

By the next day the younger son was tired and hungry.

'I shall have to find a job to earn some money,' he said.

He went to look for work on a farm, but the only job he could find was looking after the pigs.

He didn't earn much — not even enough to buy his food. He could have eaten the pig food, he felt so hungry.

Then suddenly one day, as he fed the pigs, he said to himself, 'I must be crazy. On my father's farm even the servants have more than enough to eat.

'I know what I'll do. I'll go back home and I'll tell my dad that I'm really sorry for what I've done. I'll ask if I can work for him as a servant. I'm not fit to be his son any more.'

Every day, from the day his younger
son had left, the father had looked down
the winding road towards the city,
hoping he would come back.

When at last he saw his son coming, he ran down the road to welcome him. He threw his arms around him.

'We'll have a party to celebrate,' the father said, and called the servants to bring clean clothes and a gold ring.

The older son had been working late in the fields. He heard the music and he asked the servants what the party was for.

'It's for your brother,' they said. 'Your father thought he was lost. He was afraid he was dead. But he's come back safe and sound.'

The older brother stood outside the
house and sulked.

'That's not fair,' he said. 'He should be
punished for wasting all that money, not
rewarded with a party.'

The father came out and put his arm around his older son.

'You know I love you. I don't know what I would have done without you. But your brother has come back alive. Of course I must celebrate.'

Jesus said to the teachers of God's Law, 'Do you understand? God loves you. He is glad that you do as he says and live to please him. But he is full of joy when one of his disobedient sons comes back to the kingdom.'

The Lion Story Bible is made up of 52 individual stories for young readers, building up an understanding of the Bible as one story — God's story — a story for all time and all people.

The New Testament section (numbers 31–52) covers the life and teaching of God's Son, Jesus. The stories are about the people he met, what he did and what he said. Almost all we know about the life of Jesus is recorded in the four Gospels — Matthew, Mark, Luke and John. The word gospel means 'good news'.

The last four stories in this section are about the first Christians, who started to tell others the 'good news', as Jesus had commanded them — a story which continues today all over the world.

The story of the two brothers, often called the parable of the lost or prodigal son, comes from the New Testament, Luke's Gospel, chapter 15. This chapter tells three stories about things or people that are lost: the lost sheep, the lost coin and the lost son.

Jesus said that he came to our world to seek out and to save 'the lost'. That means anyone who has gone his or her own way instead of staying close to God. In the end, going our own way makes us very unhappy. But it is never too late to 'come to our senses' like the younger son. We can come back to God and say we are truly sorry. The story shows how happy God is, just like the boy's father, to welcome us home again.

The next book in the series, number 41: *The story of the great feast*, is another of Jesus' parables. It tells what happens when God sends out an invitation.